How To Sell To Retail Chain Stores: Finding a Manufacturer's Representative

For manufacturers, importers, inventors, or anyone with a product or service to sell.

Michael Ford

GET YOUR FREE AUDIO BONUS:
See the Appendix for information on obtaining your free audio bonus.

Any examples of income are for illustration purposes only. Nothing in this book is a guarantee of income. Actual income can be more or less depending upon your efforts, the quality of your product or service, and the efforts and experience of your sales people. Some examples use estimates which are for illustrative purposes only. Nothing in this book should be considered legal or accounting advice. If you require legal or accounting advice, contact a licensed attorney or accountant.

How To Sell To Retail Chain Stores: Finding a Manufacturer's Representative

ISBN13: 978-0-9841584-9-2

The greatest teacher is first-hand experience...but sometimes it takes her several tries.

Useful Resources

Find out how you can hire freelance workers to create websites, record audio books and training courses, create software, do language translation and more.

Outsourcing Secrets Video Course
Available at
http://www.hire-me-network.com/killer-profits-outsourcing.htm

Discover the secret to importing goods from China in this special report written by someone who has done it.

Wholesale Case Study - How you can profit by importing products - eBook
Available at
http://www.elitemindsinc.com/shop/

How To Sell to Retail Chain Stores: Finding a Manufacturer's Representative

Introduction

Are you looking for a Manufacturer's Representative? Beware!

You'd better know how the system works before you take that first step.

I will tell you how selling to big companies and to retail chains using a manufacturer's representative really works so you can start selling your products today and avoid the traps that waste the time and money of those who do not understand the system.

A manufacturer's representative is someone who sells your product to major chain stores. In the simplest terms, he is a freelance salesman who represents many products.

If you have a product, you are an importer, a manufacturer, you provide a service, or even if you have a self published book, you can find a manufacturer's representative, or rep for short, to represent your product. These are sales people who visit the big retail buyers and the small ones too. They also make sales calls on industry businesses like industrial manufacturers, dentist offices, locksmith stores and any business that needs a product to solve a problem they have or a service to make their businesses work faster, cheaper, or smoother. These manufacturer's reps have an advantage you do not. They know who to talk to and what to say. They have existing relationships with many companies already who trust them and are willing to buy from them. If you have only one product then no major chain store will even talk to you. If you are not known to a company's CEO, then you are unlikely to get anything more than voicemail and he will see you as nothing more than another salesman. You need a rep to offer your product because a rep can reach the right people.

Now you may be asking "Great, where do I find these reps?" There are a number of websites that offer search services, but before you fork over anywhere from $100 to $5000 to one of these sites you need to understand how they work, which are worth the money and which are not, and how to tell the difference.

I have already been down this road. I sold my products online for years. Then I decided it was time to move into the big leagues and sell through retail stores. I faced the same problems I expect you are facing:

1. Who do I contact?
2. What do I say?
3. How do I price my product?
4. What is it going to cost me?
5. How do I know if they are taking advantage of me because I am new to this?

And a thousand other questions were racing through my head when I was told by a $250/hour consultant that I needed a manufacturer's rep. At first I tried to sell to companies myself. I quickly realized that was not going to work. No one wanted to talk to me and when they did they gave me a generic sheet of information which basically said "Send a sample and we will let you know if we like it." I sent out many samples and never heard anything back. I sent out flyers to over a hundred regional bookstores and no one responded. Only later did I find out that most samples are never even inspected. They are given out to the employees as gifts or thrown away. Big and small chain stores alike receive a room full of "samples" every day and most do not bother looking through them. Where do they find their products? Through salespeople, or reps who represent major companies or many small companies.

If you have searched for sales reps online then you know by now there are two types of listings. The free listing which is of questionable value and the paid search service which is expensive, usually $99 a month or more. The free listing is some guy you found on a message board. Is he good or not? How can you tell what he is saying is true? There are clear clues to look for that will quickly tell you which reps are good and which will make your company look like a two-bit operation. You never want one of these lame reps walking into a major chain headquarters like Wal-Mart and making your product look bad by a poor demonstration, by sounding illiterate, or by acting crazy! Yes, there are reps out there who go through the motions but know nothing about sales and some who have no people skills whatsoever. There are also about 20% of them who actually know what they are doing and 10% who can get results. Now your task is to find these good ones while avoiding the bad ones.

I will explain exactly how I did it and how you can too.

You can find manufacturer's reps, reviews of the top rep sites, and updates to this book at our private site just for buyers of this book. Go to our private page now and download a free bonus guide plus find reviews of the top manufacturer's rep sites. Go to our private site now to check it out:

http://www.Manufacturing-Rep-Secrets.com/private.html

This is the information I did not reveal in print. I have not published my manufacturer's rep website reviews in this book because they may change, some may go out of business, I may add more sites, and some of them are not very flattering. Check the above website for the latest information and links.

Selling To Salespeople

You must show a rep why he should represent your product.

Before a rep can sell your product or service to a major buyer, you must first sell the idea of your product to the rep. You must convince the rep your product is great, of interest to the public(or a specific industry sector) and is something that they can sell and make money selling. Keep in mind they know sales-speak so keep it low key, nothing over the top otherwise they may start to see you as a stereotypical used-car salesman and distrust you.

How does it work?

Usually the manufacturer's rep handles the retail buyer as his own customer. If your rep went to Walgreens HQ and they wanted 1000 units, he would take the order then pass the paperwork to you(the manufacturer) for shipping. The manufacturer would bill Walgreens directly and when they paid, the manufacturer would pay the rep's commission. If Walgreens doesn't pay, the rep gets to complain to them. If Walgreens didn't receive an order on time they would complain to the rep and the rep would complain to you(the manufacturer). Basically a rep acts as a salesperson and then a middle-man.

When Walgreens is ready for another order, they notify the rep and he lets the manufacturer know, usually by sending a completed formal order either by fax or email. It is important to have something you can print out with a date to prove the order was made so do not rely on a friendly phone order.

Get it in writing! At least send a written confirmation that references your phone conversation in response so you have some proof that you talked and an order was placed and the terms for that order.

Having the rep act as a middle-man means he always knows how many orders are made because of his sales efforts. He would not want to make a sale to Walgreens and then have them order directly from you in the future because that would take away his commissions and taking away his commissions means he is not going to sell your product to CVS Pharmacy or any other major chains.

Dealing with big chains can be a little different than dealing with smaller chains or individual stores. When dealing with big chains, like Walgreens or BestBuy, I may be forced to deal more directly with them and not through a middle-man because they use software buying systems which notify the manufacturer directly when an order needs to be filled. These systems often allow the rep to receive copies of orders too. The procedure varies from company to company.

The same approach works if the rep sells smaller numbers of a product but in those cases the rep might just buy from you directly and resell at a markup to the end user. For example, the rep would buy 10 units from the manufacturer at the agreed wholesale price, lets say $10 is the wholesale price and your retail is $30, and he would sell those 10 units for $20 a unit to a school or nursing home. He now makes more than he would selling on commission, he deals with the end buyer, and he can give a price break while still making money for everyone.

Choosing a Rep

It is important to choose the right rep for your business. Any rep cannot represent any business anymore than any coach can coach a professional baseball team.

Beware of people impersonating manufacturing reps. Sometimes you sign up for these pay services which offer listings of manufacturer's reps and receive responses from people who are not actually sales reps. They may pretend to be a rep or they may come right out and list that they are a consultant. You see these types on free message boards a lot.

If you see a generic message board posting or sign up for a pay service and immediately receive a response, within 24 hours from someone who has almost no information in his profile but makes vague statements like "I can help you sell your product" that is likely a consultant. If you receive a contact request within 24 hours of signing up and the person claims he sells to everyone, everywhere and has selected every category available in his profile claiming it is something he represents, in every region, and he sells all possible products, that is very fishy.

No real rep is going to sell everything to everyone everywhere. Any real salesperson knows that is bunk. The rep who sales medical supplies does not also sell industrial farm equipment. This is a consultant who has spammed the site search feature by selecting every possible option and dumping hot keywords in his profile. They will contact you or hope you find them and think they are playing in the big leagues when in fact they are only good at selling to people like you who need a consultant and do not understand how the system works. You think you are dealing with someone who will make sales, but this person only offers hit-or-miss advice and may not even know what he is talking about.

Now I am not saying these people are all dishonest either. You may need a consultant and they may be able to help you. But, if they are a consultant, they should never appear to be, or pretend to be a rep. If you ever contact someone who is supposed to be a manufacturer's rep and he wants you to pay him, then he is not a rep. Reps work on commission, not for up-front fees.

If you are a small company, then you have no reason to pay a rep to do hourly work. If he is really good and can represent your product well, he will start as a commission rep and once he has a series of clients he may point to his good work and ask you to take him on as a full-time salary rep. However, if he is really good, it is unlikely he would want to do this because good salespeople can make more in commission than they can make with a fixed salary. I only use commission reps and avoid any rep who wants to be paid hourly. Reps like that need to find jobs with big corporations if they need the security of a regular paycheck.

Many rep agencies with multiple reps do pay a salary, but that is between the agency and their workers. You as a manufacturer or importer should only pay a commission rate to the agency.

> *This is not a rep story, but it illustrates the point well. I once hired a computer programmer who worked by the hour. He would send me a beta version of a program, I would test it and send a list of things that needed to be corrected. He would wait a few days and send me a new version and a bill with a promise that everything is working. When I tested the new*

version, he had only fixed half of the problems I sent and most of those were obvious problems he should have seen and fixed before sending me the first beta copy. It was also obvious that simple features were not working and any testing would have shown him this fact. I would send him a new list of fixes which contained most of the old fixes and again in a few days he would send me a new version and a new bill for the hours he supposedly spent working on it, but the new version only fixed half of the remaining problems. It was obvious he was taking me for a ride. He sent me code he knew was full of bugs because he knew I would send a list of fixes and he could charge me more hours to fix the problems he should have fixed weeks earlier. I never hire a programmer or a rep to work by the hour. A programmer should work for a flat fee and a rep should work for a percentage commission.

It may not always be a consultant who contacts you, but someone who is trying to scam you, a pseudo-rep. These people pretend to be big time rep agencies, but in fact, they only want one of two things: either they want an up-front commission, or they will try to farm out your job to other reps on the same website or on other sites. It is a type of arbitrage where the pseudo-rep tries to make a 20% commission deal with you and then pretends to be the manufacturer to another real rep for 10%. This pseudo-rep is hoping to make 10% off of everything the real rep sells while you think the pseudo-rep is the one doing the work when he is only passing messages. These types of arrangements usually fall through and the pseudo-rep does nothing but waste your time, make endless promises, and eventually disappears when he realizes he is not going to make easy money from you. The warning signs are the same as for a consultant: making too many promises, telling you exactly what you want to hear, representing every sector, every product, every region. Avoid anyone who does everything and exactly what you want. That rep is promising too much.

Commissions

This is the big question, what does it cost. You have to pay your rep something to sell for you. If you pay too little, he will have no interest in selling. If you pay too much, you are giving away your profits or your price becomes too high for retailers to buy your product.

Commissions vary from 5% to 20% or more depending on your product. You may have been hoping to pay 5% or 10%, but good salespeople expect to be paid for their time and will not be interested in representing products they cannot make money selling. Many expect 20%. Since this is the case, tell them you are glad to pay 20% and raise your product wholesale price to them so you make the same amount and they can charge 20%. Of course, you do not tell them you are charging a higher price, but they should know it anyway.

> *Example: If the wholesale price of your product is $10,000.00 then a 5% commission is 500.00 which is not bad. If a rep can sell it easily he might be interested, but 10% would make him more interested.*
>
> *If your product is $2 wholesale, then no rep will care about a 5% commission unless he can sell 10,000 or more at the time.*

So you will have to create multiple price lists, one for 10% commissions, one for 15%, one for 20% and if your item is a high profit product maybe a 25% rate sheet. Now when your rep says he charges 10%, you can send a 10% commission price sheet. If he charges 20%, send the 20% sheet.

If your product can sell retail for $10 and you can make it for $0.25 that gives you a lot more latitude in your pricing than if your product retails for $20 and it costs you $8.

Some high volume products like soft drinks may have a 4% commission if your rep sees potential in the line and knows it will be reordered in high volume. A commission of 4% to 10% is common for food products that will be reordered regularly. If your product has a wholesale cost of $10 then it is unlikely any rep would care about a 5% commission unless he thought he could sell thousands at a time. It is unlikely any rep would consider a 5% commission unless he knew the product would fly off the shelves with little sales effort.

However, if you are selling high priced items or you are a distributor then you are likely not selling at a true wholesale price. Here is how it works for car sales. If you have a car lot and sell cars that cost $45,000.00 list price then the profit is around $8,000 for the dealer because the invoice price is 45000-8000=$37,000. Salesmen are then paid based on this markup above the invoice price, not the total price. Most car salesmen make 20% to 25% and that is only on the markup, not the full price which would be $1600 at 20% for a $45,000 vehicle sold at list price(20% of $8000 is $1600).

If you sell high priced industrial or medical equipment, or any similar highly specialized product, you most likely need your own trained sales force instead of a rep who sells many products. You might still use a manufacturer's rep to find interested clients and pay a finder's fee if you make a sale. The rep should understand how payments work and that his job is to find customers and let your sales team take over with the product details. A rep who makes calls to medical companies could feel them out and let you know if they need your product. He can possibly warm the waters of interest with a brochure or big promise and then say someone higher up than him will call the clinic with more details at a convenient time. Most reps will be interested in products they can sell for a commission and not bother with anything else that involves complicated payments though.

It is important to know what commission rate a rep expects. If a rep expects a 20% and you tell him you pay a 10%, then he may give a generic answer and turn you down. You never know why because he does not tell you that his firm does not represent products for less than 20% commissions. You need to ask what the rep's commission rate is FIRST. Then you will have a sheet already prepared for that rate(as previously described).

A new or less experienced rep may not know what rate he should charge so you can mention 10% or 15%. He may take it. If you do not hear back from the rep or if he turns you down, then recontact later and offer a 20% commission with a new price sheet that simply has higher wholesale prices. You can always say you talked to other reps and found out they were asking 20% so you thought your first offer was too low. Of course, in reality you only raised your wholesale price, but he does not know that. You make the same amount on each purchase and the rep still makes a 20% commission.

Always find out your rep's desired commission rate FIRST, then send your pricing. NEVER send your pricing and then ask the reps rates.

Your wholesale cost is determined by the rep's rate. A rep who wants a higher commission gets a sheet with higher prices. A rep willing to work for a lower rate gets lower prices.

Something else you must think about is oversells. This is when your rep sells your product for more than you expected. If a rep maintains his own warehouse he can do this and cut you out of the loop. He will simply order 1000 of product X at $10 and then sell it to a local retailer for $15.00. Now what does he make? He makes your 10% commission of $1 per unit plus the $5 markup so he makes $6 per unit profit. You never know about his extra profit or the fact that a buyer is willing to pay more because you are shipping directly to the rep's warehouse and he is acting as a distributor. I prefer reps who do not maintain their own warehouse but sometimes it is good for a rep to warehouse items that are very small or very large. You can't begrudge a rep extra profit from this type of sale either. They make what they can make. But, you need to be on top of pricing and you need to know if retail outlets are willing to pay more than your listed wholesale price. You may be priced too low.

So what do you do to encourage reps to sell at a higher price? Simple, offer an alternate commission or a split with them. If they sell your $10 wholesale product for $15 then they get the commission plus 50% of the oversell. That is a great deal and most reps will consider it fair plus you both make more money than you would have otherwise. This only matters if the oversell is a significant amount. If they are overselling your product by $1 or $2 then just pay the commission on that and don't worry about splitting anything.

Why offer a 20% commission?

You will find better quality reps by offering an attractive commission. Inexperienced reps may take whatever you offer because they do not know the market rates or do not believe they can negotiate.

Offering a higher commission gives you an advantage. Suppose your rep already represents one of your competitors who is paying 10% or 15%. If your product is as good or even slightly better and you are offering the same rate then the rep has no reason to learn a new product. If you pay a 20% commission, the rep may quietly stop representing the other product and start representing yours. If you are the first manufacturer to offer a rep at 20% and your competitor comes along later asking to distribute his product, your rep will have no problem turning him down when your competitor offers a 10% commission.

Setting Your Wholesale Price

When setting your wholesale price, you generally want 2x to 3x your total production costs back on each sale as an ABSOLUTE MINIMUM. Don't forget to include all of your expenses, not just material expenses, when calculating your cost per product. Just because your product uses two-cents in plastic does not mean it costs two-cents to make. You have to pay someone to run a $10k machine (which you are making payments on) to form that plastic, rent, and other expenses. The 2x or 3x rule is not absolute. If your product costs 25 cents to produce and you can sell it wholesale for $15, go for it! The price is based on what the market will bear, not the minimum you need to make. Don't give your product away just because you can afford to do so or because you think it will generate more sales. People buy because they "want" not because something is cheap. No one ever bought two outdoor grills at the same time because they were $2 each and no one ever walked out of a store refusing to pay $60 for a grill while muttering that they were not paying more than $54. If they want it, they pay it, as long as it is within reason.

When it comes to price testing, start low and then raise your price in a test market to see at what price you make the most PROFIT(not the most sales). If you start high and then try to lower the price, everyone will complain, "I paid $10 last week and now the price is $7, can I get a $3 per unit credit now". If you start low and raise the price, no one complains about past purchases. Make sure to test prices on a limited market first, not on everyone.

Remember, you want more than one price sheet. The price sheets should be for 10%, 15% and 20% commissions. Each has wholesale prices adjusted so that you make about the same after the commission. When you encounter a rep who works for 20% normally, send him the 20% list of prices and mark in your notes that he is a 20% guy(in case you have to send updates or make price changes later, you do not want to send him a 10% sheet and then find out he has been selling at those prices and now wants a 20% cut, plus he might be upset if you then corrected your error and raised prices on him.)

Getting Paid

There are various ways companies can pay you. Small stores or even small chains may pay by Visa/MC which is fine and so is a check. I do prefer prepayment but will do Net 30/60 as long as I do not have too much of an outstanding investment in the merchandise sent to one store. Net 30/60 would mean you and your rep both wait 30/60 days for payment so try to get prepayments. Shipping is usually invoiced with the product and is not part of the commission calculation. Shipping is not included in the wholesale prices. If someone pays by check and it does not cover the shipping amount, I have been adjusting the quantity down until the amount paid covers the shipping+product.

Finding The Right Rep

Always talk to a rep on the phone before agreeing to anything. You want to hear what he or she sounds like and remember: that is the voice that will represent your product. Is the rep's English broken, does he or she use bad grammar, curse inappropriately, sound uneducated? Then you do not want that person representing your product.

When you are using the online websites which list reps, look at the posting made by the rep. What does he say and how does he say it? Some warning signs are postings in ALL CAPITAL LETTERS. This is a clear sign of someone who is inexperienced with computers. If they send a follow-up email to a retail buyer are they going to SCREAM THROUGH THE ENTIRE EMAIL? Yes, they will and it will make you and your product look bad. The retail buyer will think this sales rep is an idiot and you must be too if you are using him. Avoid anyone who SCREAMS in their information posting.

Look for good grammar and proper punctuation. If a rep posts his own information to potential clients and uses bad grammar then you can be sure he will use bad grammar in all other communications too.

Here is an example of a posting from a rep that I avoided.

> " i have retail sales experience, so i have great customer service. i like helping people out either help them save money, or just voluntary help out. also, i have some outside sales, such as merchant sales, medical equipment sales, and direct sales. i'm here to find a good opportunity, so i can grow with the company"

Notice how he started with a space, then a lower case I. He spliced his sentences with commas and never used the shift key once. He throws in random commas, in case his comma splices are not enough, and there is no ending punctuation. I guess he got tired of using so much punctuation by the end of the paragraph so he quit. His sentences make little sense. I would never want this person representing my company.

Here is another rep who lost any chance of representing my product because he SCREAMED EVERYTHING:

> " FOR ABOUT EIGHTEEN (18) YEARS (1980-1998), SOLD VARIOUS BANKING SERVICES WHILE WORKING WITH A MULTINATIONAL BANK. GOT MY ASSOCIATE DEGREE IN BANKING DURING THIS PERIOD.
>
> VENTURED INTO THE IT FIELD (WIDE AREA NETWORKING) IN 2000 AND BECAME CERTIFIED AS A MICROSOFT CERTIFIED

ASSOCIATE - TCP/IP. THEN ALSO IN 2001 I PASSED MY EXAMS TO BECOME A CISCO CERTIFIED NETWORK ASSOCIATE (CCNA).

BEEN IN GENERAL MERCHANDISING SIDE BY SIDE. I PAY ATTENTION TO DETAIL, I EASILY ADJUST TO PROGRESSIVE CHANGE. I HOLD INTEGRITY IN THE HIGHEST ESTEEM AND I EXPECT PEOPLE I DEAL WITH TO BE PEOPLE OF INTEGRITY."

His sentences make no sense. He starts with a blank space then in the first line he omits the word "I" and uses a comma instead. He splices sentences with commas instead of using the correct punctuation. This is a clear sign of laziness and I do not want someone who is too lazy to use proper grammar and too dumb to use proper capitalization to represent my product to retail stores. In the last paragraph he starts with "BEEN IN" instead of saying "I have been in" and the sentence would make no sense even if he started it correctly. I also cannot believe this person is honestly in any IT field. If he was, and if he knew anything about using computers or net-etiquette, he would not SCREAM so much.

Here is another example of a real rep's profile that the rep typed himself or herself:

CARD & GIFT STORES,TOY STORES,DRUG STORES,STATIONARY STORES,KIDS ACCESSORY STORES, HOSPITAL GIFT SHOPS, COLLEGE BOOK STORES, CANDY SHOPS , SOUVENIR STORES,GARDEN CENTERS & SEA SHORE STORES ETC.

LINES: GNERAL GIFTS, TOYS,

STATIONARY & CARDS, KIDS NOVELTIES
, SOUVENIRS,BATH PRODUCTS, GARDEN
CENTER MDSE ETC.

Look at this closely. He misspelled General as GNERAL, he throws commas between two spaces " , " some places and butts words up against a comma with no space in others. HE SHOUTS CONSTANTLY. Do you want someone like this representing your product? If he emails a retail buyer, what is the buyer going to think when he receives a SHOUTING EMAIL full of such obvious mistakes? That buyer will have no interest in your product and reps like this can poison buyers opinions of your product if they remember your brand name when another rep comes calling. They may assume it was YOU contacting them the first time and not a rep which makes you look illiterate. Never use a rep who cannot write like an educated adult.

Here is another example from a real rep's profile:

CUSTOMERS: I service about 200 convinience and liquor stores in SFO bay area.

LINES: Any items which can be used inside convinience and liquor stores

Notice how this person misspelled convenience. How is it possible this is his main market yet he does not know how to spell it? Do you want this person emailing a convenience store buyer on your behalf with such a silly error in the email? Watch for warning signs like this.

Here is yet another one from a real rep's profile:

CUSTOMERS: We a an extreamly deversefied compant sellint to any available customerlocated in the state of New Jersey.

This person misspelled more words than he spelled correctly. Is he serious? Is this what his resume looks like? That is exactly what this posting is, a resume. He is asking me to pay him a commission to do a job. He wants to work for me and this is how little he thinks of me? You have to wonder what some of these people are thinking. Do they really expect companies to hire them as representatives with communication skills like these? And, yes this is a REAL posting by a REAL person trying to act as a rep. I do not know how many companies he represents, but I feel bad for them all. This person also does not list real customers in the CUSTOMERS: area which is dumb. I cannot judge whether he reaches my target customers or not because I have no idea who he contacts. Instead of saying who his customers are, he gives a sales pitch, a bad one. No one can find him based on a search keyword(unless they grossly misspell it). He tries to appeal to everyone. That is another warning sign. Any rep who can sell to "anyone" is only dreaming. Any real rep has a specific market or a few specific markets, but no one can sell to "anyone". This person also is clearly lazy, ignorant, and incompetent. He posted one sentence and did not bother to proofread it or if he did proofread it he still posted it with the errors. Either way, he is not suitable to represent any company. Never waste your time with reps like this.

Here is another posting from a rep:

> CUSTOMERS: Businesses 20 - 500 employees
>
> LINES: Advertising/marketing SEO Print and Mail Services TV Commercial Production ad placement Sales Training Operational and Management Training

I found this one simply confusing. Is he offering a service for advertising/marketing to me as a manufacturer/importer with 20-500 employees or is he offering to sell my advertising/ marketing related service to businesses of 20-500 employees? His posting is not very clear and that makes me suspect he is not a rep at all but a consultant pretending to be a rep or even someone trying to sell advertising to manufacturers. I would not trust him.

Judge reps from their websites.

A rep's website can tell you a lot about the rep. How professional is he, does his site look like a 12 year old threw it together or does it look like a real business site?

Not all reps have websites, but today most do. Watch out for reps who do not have real websites. When I say they do not have a *real* website I mean they have a webpage on a free hosting service that has pop up ads or they have a free Google hosted service or they have their webpage on a personal account for aol.com or verizon.net which looks like www3. users.verizon.net/johnsmith901. If any company cannot pay a few dollars for a hosting account and a domain name, then that company is not a company and the person pretending to be a company is not serious about doing business. This applies to ANY business on the Internet too. Anyone offering a business service who is too cheap or too dumb to register a domain and pay a few dollars a month for hosting is not making any money or is incompetent. Avoid them. I found one consultant masquerading as a rep and when I went to her website she claimed to have "Management of sales reps in 50 states", whatever "management of sales reps" is supposed to mean, but her site was hosted for free on Google. The website looked like a free template she downloaded from a the web, one of those sites that gives away templates because they are too poor in quality to sell. She did not even have a real domain name registered and used an aol.com address for her email. I did not waste my time on this one. Anyone who is serious about his or her business will register a domain and pay for real webhosting. The page may not be fancy, but anyone who is serious will have a real hosting account and not a free one.

Here is an example of a consultant posting on a manufacturer's rep listing service:

> CUSTOMERS: We call on ALL customers that fit your business. We are a FULL SERVICE AGENCY. We make sales, service accounts, and do resets. Let us help you grow your business.
>
> LINES: We make sales, service accounts, and do resets. Let us help you grow your business. Our core business is the Building Material Industry. We deal with Independent and BIG BOX stores.

Notice how he does everything everywhere and wants to help me "grow" my business. All warning signs. This posting shows that he does not target any customers(none listed) and he has no lines(none listed, just a sales pitch in its place). They are a consultancy. They say they do not require an up-front fee in the options, but they actually do. If a rep says in his profile he does not require an up-front fee and then in the first two or three emails or phone conversations he says something about a fee, drop him fast. He has dishonestly listed in his profile he does not require a fee and now he does. Do not trust people like this. If you want a consultant then these postings are what you want to look for, but make sure they are honest in the posted information and are not pretending to be a rep and not claiming to be fee-free then demanding a fee.

Some other warning signs are people who use MSN.com or AOL.com or webtv.com email addresses. People who use AOL.com as their main Internet service are generally considered....ahem, let's just say less than intelligent in the world of the web. When I receive a customer support request and it is from an AOL address, I know it is going to be some doozy like "I can't get the disk to play on my TV." when they bought a software CD. People who use AOL instead of a real service provider are inexperienced and likely to have silly problems that make them look dumb. When a rep knows so little about the web that he uses AOL.com as his email address, or uses AOL.com at all, it makes me question his ability.

As a manufacturer, you should have your own website and use your domain name as your email address. The same applies to reps. To do anything else is a sign of incompetence or laziness. Using your own domain name is much more professional than using an AOL.com, MSN.com or gmail.com or or hotmail.com other free email service address. The email can be directed to these services, but the people sending you email should never see the domain name of your ISP or free mail service. It is common for people to register a domain name, then use gmail.com to actually read their email because it is a nice interface. But, you can setup your account so it only sends and receives email using your registered company domain name, not gmail.com or any other free service name.

Beware of any rep who is clearly spamming keywords in his profile. If you search for a rep or one contacts you and in his profile you see long lists of keywords and many of them are unrelated to the others, this is a sign the person is not a real rep but a consultant. He is spamming his listing with keywords knowing that eventually you will search on one of those hot topic keywords and contact him so he can tell you how great his services are and how much he will charge you to make you rich. If a consultant spams keywords and does not admit he is a consultant in his listing, then he has already restored to dishonest advertising to draw you in. Do not trust him.

Here is an example of a keyword spammer:

> Customers: business to business, information technology, hardware, software, computers, Microsoft, Lenovo, HP, printers, servers, backup, solutions, wireless, keyboards, mice, switches, routers, networking, web design, media, accessories, systems, workstations, notebooks, laptops, desktops, remote, security, Adobe, Symantec, McAfee, VMware, Dell, retail, apparel, gift shop, medical, OEM, industrial, machine, component, auto, department store, distributor, wholesale, hospital, insurance, real estate, small business, engineering, government, reseller, education, hospitality, mining, printing, imaging, antivirus, spyware, operating systems, linux, Windows XP, windows vista, apple, Internet, web hosting,

Here, he lists completely unrelated items from computer software to real estate to government. Also notice how the ends the list with a dangling comma. All clear signs of a person to avoid.

If you sell automotive products and a rep contacts you who lists only medical products, do not send him a message saying Not-A-Match or ignore him immediately. You never know what he REALLY sells. He may have listed one aspect of the business or he may have expanded since that profile was posted. If a rep is interested in you(and they are not an obvious consultant) it is always in your interest to at least ask how he can represent your product. You never know what other ideas or projects a rep may have. Maybe his brother owns a chain of car dealerships! If you find out he is a consultant wanting to charge you or not a match, you do not have to go any farther. Maybe they are interested in expanding into your field, maybe they did not list their full profile, maybe they do not want to reveal how big their operation is, but reps interested in you who contact you directly are at least worth talking to.

Worldwide Sales

There are reps who specialize in selling products in other countries. This can open up new markets you would have never considered. Perhaps your product would be hot in Japan or South Africa. You have no contacts there and you may not even speak Japanese. You can find a rep who will promote your product in other countries and greatly expand your market.

The idea of selling your product around the world can be appealing, but you must think about what that really means before you make a deal. Are there any safety or other laws you will have to comply with? Your rep may or may not know about them. How will you ship your product and what will it cost? You may make money shipping your product in the USA, but shipping a pallet to Germany may cost more in shipping than the product is worth retail. You may not be able to ship cost effectively unless you can sell a shipping container(about the size of a semi-trailer) full of goods. Can you sell that much to one customer? You need to know this before you make a deal for 100,000 units or even 10 units to be shipped to Germany.

You may have never thought about selling internationally because you do not speak Japanese or Chinese. How could you possible sell in these countries with zero knowledge of their markets and when you cannot even talk to your buyers? That is where a rep saves the day. There are many reps who specialize in specific countries. You never have to talk to the retail buyer because your rep will do that.

We are more forgiving on English grammar rules when it comes to international reps. It is more important they speak their own language well and not as important they speak English well.

Your rep will also know the customs, what is hot, and what is not. He can even suggest product changes and packaging changes to make your product appeal to another country. When searching for a rep, use keywords for major countries like Japan. You do not want to forget smaller countries either. These smaller countries are not the first thing on the minds of marketers, but for a small manufacturer, one good account in a small country of a few million people could be a huge boom to your business plus you may have no competition in a small country.

I will warn you in advance that some of these "reps" are actually consulting firms. However it may be worthwhile to pay them if they really can help you market your product in another country and introduce you to real reps.

Ask for references! You want to know that they can do what they promise. What other products have they represented and where are those products selling. Also verify the reference is a real company and not the rep's brother or secretary. Watch for success. If they cannot deliver, then do not keep paying them. Do not make any large up-front payments either. If they charge a $3000.00 "retainer" then how do you know they will not simply take your money and change their phone number? Always pay as you go even if it costs more in the long run.

Now you may be thinking that even if you have a rep you are a one man operation and cannot redesign your label and manuals in Chinese. Again, there is a simple solution. You can easily outsource those jobs and hire a freelancer for a very small amount to rewrite your manual. You can even hire someone who is a native speaker and can make suggestions you might not have thought about. All you do is send this person the text on your label or brochure in a .doc file, they send you back the translation, then you copy and paste that into your design software and work with it until it looks good. Then send a digital copy of the final version to your rep to check for you. You should also have someone else, other than the person who did the original translation, check your translation. Your rep may not check it as closely as he could and a second set of eyes is always a good idea. If you need a translator or someone to design your box, visit the special link in the appendix where we provide links and more information on how to outsource such jobs for much less than you might expect.

Big Chain Nightmares

Big chains are where manufacturers wants to sell their product. They salivate when they think about their product being on thousands of Wal-Mart or K-Mart shelves. The unfortunate fact is that these chains are unlikely to talk to you or your rep. If they do take an interest in your product, you may regret it. They will nickel and dime you for every cent they can trim off the price. They will dangle a 1000 unit order in your face and then make you come down so low you make a penny per unit while they make you feel guilty for that much profit. You may make what you think is a good deal and then realize you are paying for shipping costs, storage fees at THEIR warehouse, advertising fees for THEIR newspaper ads, and other fees you never heard of. You are much better off with smaller chains and even individual stores. These are more likely to accept the price you give them without question. They are also a better place to start because the entry bar is lower, they have fewer manufacturers or reps knocking on their door and they need good products not sold at the big chains.

The first time a rep contacted me I did not even know what one was. He said he represented K-Mart, Wal-Mart and some other major drug chains. He wanted to know what my software pricing was and said he was looking for something around $2.50 a unit. What a joke! That is my cost. Even if I sold to him at double that price I would be making so little money it would not be worth shipping the products. If I sold 1000 units I only make 2500.00 profit at double the price he quoted. I can sell 100 units through my website and make the same money for less work. If I could sell that many units a day or even a week I might consider it, but that was *not realistic and besides, there is no way he would double his price. If I dealt with him I would lose money on every order just for the thrill of doing business with the "Big Boys". Always do the math and see if it is worth your time to sell anything. Do not make an agreement just because you make some small profit. Keep the quality of your product in mind. If a big chain will not pay what it is worth, then sell to 10 small stores that will. If you are already selling to the small chains and cut a big chain a great deal just to get in the store, you may lose those 10 small chains because they will no longer be able to compete. When they see the big chain selling the same product for a price that is the same as they pay wholesale, they will feel cheated too. You will alienate the stores that are making you money just to get an unsteady foothold in one big store. That big store may also drop you anytime so it is never a certain money maker.*

Do Your Own Selling

Just because you have a rep does not mean you cannot sell your product yourself. Contact local stores. Get your local phone book and setup appointments. Speak at local civic groups about the benefits of using your product or about your industry and how it is changing or just give them some good advice that is related to your industry and tell them three or ten things they can do to improve their lives that are related to your industry. It can be an opportunity to network with influential people in local businesses.

You can find contact information for businesses around the US and in Canada in a catalog of retail stores. It will give you a better feel for the retail business and you may find selling directly to stores is something you can do yourself.

Let your rep sell around the country and you can visit retail buyers in your local state. This is especially good for you because while your rep visits big chains, you can go to small stores your rep might not bother with. You can find a link to this 1000+ page chain store listing with full contact information at

http://www.Manufacturing-Rep-Secrets.com/private.html

Tracking

Keep track of your contacts. You can never expect to remember all of your reps. You may easily have 10 or 20 or 100 or more. You will need some way to keep track of them. It can be a text file or fancy software like Outlook or ACT Contact Manager, and gmail.com and yahoo.com both have free online contact managers. There are many people trackers or contact managers out there that you can use. You will want to enter notes every time you communicate with a salesperson. Make a note about the time, date, what you talked about, what you are going to do next, and anything personal the rep said, like the name of his wife, kids, dog etc. Make sure you do whatever it is you need to do next too. Making notes is no good if you do not follow up and do something. If you do not keep good notes then you may have a sales person who forgets about you and you will lose sales if you fail to notify your top sales people about new products or product changes.

Here are the notes I have on one of my new reps:

Rep Name: XXXX, Addr: XXXXXXX Phone: XXXXX, Email: XXXXXXX
NOTES: He contacted me through xxxxxxxx.com, has bookstore contacts too
I emailed him Jan 2 2010, he responded immediately asking me to call him or asking for a good time for him to call me. I called immediately and we discussed my product line and commissions of 10%. He is going to check the website and think about it.
Jan 4 2010 – Emailed me to turn down offer because he said his lines are all 20% or more. I did not send him a price sheet yet so I adjusted prices up and offered a 20% commission.
Jan 4-2010 responded by email and said would run it by his reps and get back to me at the end of the week due to the Atlanta Gift Show. Follow up if I do not hear back from him by next week.

How Many?

How many reps do you need? As many as it takes. If you have a narrow niche market product, such as the medical waste disposal industry, then there may only be a few reps qualified to deal with your product. If you have a popular product that is suitable for retail stores, you may want 100 reps. Not all will be great sellers. You need enough working so you benefit from the good ones but have the lower quality ones as filler. Every sale is still a sale and as long as they are working on commission one good salesman is as good as 10 weak ones who sell the same amount. You will also find that many reps simply sell nothing. They love the idea of bringing on a new client and product to sell, but once they have you aboard, they do not know what to do. They go to the same people they always go to and if those limited customers do not buy the product, they do not know what to do next. The idea of going to a new retail buyer never enters their head.

You will quickly identify these weak salespeople. They will make one or two sales and then no more or none ever. Add a note in your database about your experience so if they call or contact you through one of the networking sites, you know they are a dud when you look them up in your notes.

Background Checks

Most sites list an option showing whether or not a rep will submit to a background check. Some larger reps simply do not care to fool with this so they may select No. Selecting No or Yes does not really indicate anything about the rep. A new agency may select no simply because they have no history. You should do some due diligence research on anyone you hire. Do a Google search for their name and then their email and then their phone and then their address. What comes up? Remember that many people have the same name so look for anything unusual and verify it is the same person in the same city or state. Also look for other businesses they may be connected to.

In this day and age, before jumping into the business bed, you should do a thorough check. Once you have identified a rep as a possible match for your company, check out his or her history. You need to know if this person has a criminal record or has declared bankruptcy recently or if there is anything unusual about the rep.

You can find out how to do an in depth background search on our private webpage:

http://www.Manufacturing-Rep-Secrets.com/private.html

The One Sheet

The fastest method used to spread the word about your product in days gone by was personal calls, postal mailers, and a lot of face to face sales meetings. In today's digital world, a product sheet, or one-sheet, in color, one per product is the correct method. It should be both available as a printed sheet(your local copy shop can print them) and in a PDF format. It is also a good idea to save the PDF as a JPG image file. Some people still cannot figure out how to open a PDF so a JPG makes a good backup option.

You will need a single sheet(two sides) that explains what your product is and why a retailer should buy it. Below the product name, you need a catchy sub-headline that promises a benefit either from your product to the end user or to the retailer. You need to list in bullet points the benefits of your products(not just the features).

Your rep will use this when talking to a retail buyer and leave it with the buyer who may want to think about it or read over the sheet later.

Your one-sheet is a nicely printed, two sided, color page with a quality large image of your product. You can make them using any quality color printer and good quality glossy paper. On the back you will want to include customer testimonials, awards, or any other information that will give a buyer confidence in your product. You will also want to include any suggestions such as purchasing one cleaning kit for every two products because your research shows one out of two buyers also buys a cleaning kit. You can also include suggestions for related products such as garden hose accessories if you sell garden hoses. Your one-sheet should feature one product. You may want to make a grouping sheet which shows three or four related products, but you will also want individual one sheets for each product.

You can also download an editable example one sheet on our webpage in the appendix.

Your one-sheet must be appealing but not too complicated. One paragraph about the product and as many bullet points as possible is enough. If you can write the entire thing in bullet points or in two or three groups of bullet points, do it.

It does not have to be extremely fancy but should be easy to read, show a large image of your product in a flattering way, and be clear what your product does. Use the product name as the headline, not the name of your company. No one cares what your company name is unless it is a household name already. They care about the product that may or may not be on their shelves. For your bullet points make sure to stress benefits. It is great if you have features and sometimes those should be listed but make sure the benefit are clear.

It has 300 Megapixels... so what?

*It takes super high quality images with 300 Megapixel resolution which is 10 times the industry standard...*Ok, I can get excited about that because I now see the benefit to my picture taking. Now I know it takes high quality images and I know this product is far above the industry standard.

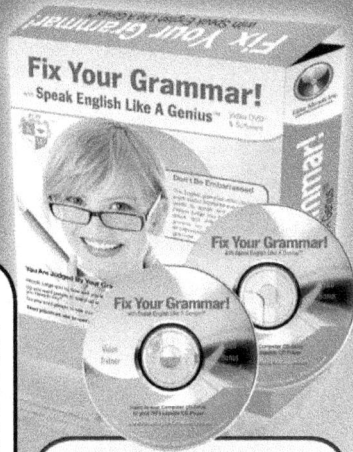

Example of the front of a one-sheet.
Download a template for this one-sheet from the website in the appendix.

You can always express your ideas more effectively when your writing is grammatically correct.

It does not matter if your are writing to friends on social websites, your blog, for your company website, writing for news and media networks, writing a client proposal, or if you are closing a big business deal with a formal letter, you need to present yourself in the best way possible, you must use good grammar or you will not be taken seriously.

RightWriter will separate your writing from those around you. No matter what your writing goals are, RightWriter can improve your writing's impact.

RightWriter is the software tool that actually improves your grammar skills.
You don't have to understand grammar rules to use RightWriter. RightWriter will show you the problem area and make suggestions explaining how to fix it.

The Final RightWriter Report Includes

• Readability Score Graphs - Shows you the Flesch Index, Flesch-Kincaid Grade Level Index and the Fog Index ratings for your document which help you improve your document's readability
• Strength Score
• Descriptive Word Score
• Jargon Index
• Sentence Structure Recommendations
• Text Statistics(Number of Words, Words per sentence, etc)
• Words To Review(And the reason you need to review them)

Example of the back of a one-sheet.
This one shows screen shots of the software and awards it has won.

Be sure to include a space where your rep can put a sticker with his contact information or you can include it as part of the design.

Use the back of each one-sheet for weights, in depth details, packaging, point of purchase display photos, awards, testimonials, etc.

NO pricing. There should be no pricing anywhere on the one-sheet.

Once the product has been on the shelf a while and you have some sales numbers, sell-through ROI and RPSF can be added to the back of your sheets. Store merchandising will be important for impact merchandising.

You should provide your rep with a pdf and .jpg format for emailing and printed versions. If you depend on your rep to print the one-sheets from his printer, he may not have a color printer or may print ugly copies or may print them on two sheets instead of one. Print your own one-sheets on a nice printer or have them professionally printed at your local copy shop. Only print in small lots. You may find you want to update or correct the page often. It is better to pay a little more per page for 50 and then update them than to pay for 500 and throw 450 in the recycle bin after you realize there is a spelling error in the title. Don't forget to put a place for the rep's contact information.

A one sheet is not a magic bullet. Do not expect to send it to a retail buyer yourself and suddenly your phone rings the next day with an order for 1000 units. This is a tool used by a salesperson who knows how to sell. It is a tool in his toolbox.

Sales Training Audio

Wouldn't it be nice if you could send a sample product to a rep, then he shows it to a retailer buyer and explains all of the features like an expert then takes an order for a million units. That is not how it really works. Some products require no explanation like scented candles, but most require some explanation or assurance they can sell. Every product requires some unique selling property that makes it different from the 20 other reps offering the same thing the retail buyer will meet with this week.

You know your product well. You know the benefits and features. You know what makes your product special or unique. Your rep does not. To your rep, it is just a box with something inside he can make 20% on. In order for your rep to properly represent your product he must know HOW to sell it. Sending him your 50 page product manual or giving him your website address is not going to work. Reps are busy, represent many products, and have little interest in becoming an expert on your product. They just need to know enough to sell it. It is unlikely a rep would bother to attend an orientation meeting as well. Besides, your rep may be in New York when you are in California. Why would a rep fly out to meet you for a couple of hours to talk about a product he may or may not actually be able to sell.

Now, how can we educate our rep so he actually understands the product and has a better chance of making sales? The answer is audio. Everyone has either an MP3 player or CD player in the car or on his phone or he carries one to listen to audio books on sales topics. If you can provide an audio book that explains your product, then your sales person will listen to it while driving to sales calls, while flying, while relaxing. Plus, you only have to hold one sales meeting with yourself and share copies of it with every rep interested in your product. It is the best way to educate reps.

First, write up everything you want a rep to know and how your product should be sold. Try not to throw in everything plus the kitchen sink. You want to keep it lean and tight. Stick to only the important parts. What three things can your sales person say to get a sale? List those. Don't list the 20 great points of your product. Put those on the back of the one-sheet. You only need your rep to remember those three things to generate a sale so he can mention them in a meeting. If you are going to record the audio yourself, you may only need an outline of what you want to say. If you are going to have someone else record the audio, you will need a full script.

Once you have your presentation written up and it includes all the important points, have it recorded to audio. You can do it yourself or you can hire someone. There are many professional and semi-professional voice artists who will read your guide and send you an audio file. If you want to know how to hire people to record audio like this, not just for this project but to develop other products and to help with your marketing, you can find out how on our private member page in the appendix. Now that you have hired a good voice person or recorded it yourself and have your audio, send it to your sales reps. You can make it available on the web so they can download it to their MP3 player immediately or send it on a CD with your rep kit.

What to include in your orientation audio program:
- Quickly describe your company, its background, the main members, why they are qualified to produce this product.
- What launched the company, an idea, a group of

college friends?

- Describe the market your products are aimed at.

- Describe any special considerations. Is your product seasonal? Is it a hot seller at Halloween only? Does your product sell well after a disaster? Can your product be customized for the retailer?

- What niche markets are good targets for your product?

- If a company orders Product A, then explain why they should also order Product B. For example, if you sell water purification systems, then the buyer should order replacement filters too(be sure to explain why, it may not be as obvious why product B is needed for your product as you think). Also make it easy on the buyer and explain how much of product B should be purchased. Does your average customer buy one water purification system and three spare filters? Then say so. Don't make the buyer think more than he has to. Tell him, "For every water purification system on the shelf, you need three replacement filter packs. This allows the customer to purchase enough filters at the same time so they do not worry about them being unavailable in the future."

- Give an example sales pitch. If you were in front of a buyer, what would you say? Show the rep how you want your product represented. Then the reps can modify that presentation to meet their needs, the needs of the buyers, or their own style.

- Tell the rep clearly what the unique selling point of your product is. Why is your product better, faster, healthier, or easier to use than any similar product.

- Explain how your product should be positioned in the store. Do you provide in store displays? Can you provide them if you do not do so now? Is your product a point of purchase product or is it better sold when placed by the camping supplies? Again, what is an obvious choice for you may not be obvious to the retailer. They may never think to put your paint remover next to the paint. They may send it to stores with no instructions and a stock boy will place it in the window glazing section because the colors are similar to other products there. Be specific.

- Discuss your competition. Why is your product better? Why is your marketing better? If you do not have an established sales history, then what is your competition's sales history? Do they sell one million units a month? Then let the rep know that could be your market because your product's unique selling property makes yours better than the competition's product.

- Make a list of common objections and give a response for each. It is too expensive, I am not going to act on it now, I will think about it, It seems too complicated, my customers are not smart enough to use it, my customers like what they have now, I am not sure it will meet my customer's needs, I already have a similar product, why don't I just buy Brand X instead, etc. You will also have specific objections for your product so include those.

- Explain any terms or conditions connected to your product, your sales, etc. If you can only sell your product in the USA, say so. If you only sell in quantities of 100, let the retailer/rep know. Here you should also explain what you expect from the rep after the sale(does the rep pass orders to you, deal with buyer problems directly? Basically, describe what the rep's role is as a representative or his role if the rep chooses to buy your product and resell directly to his/her clients.)

- Explain how orders should be handled and what you

expect from the rep. Will the rep take and forward all orders to you or will the rep only generate the first order and from then on have the buyer contact the vendor directly. How should orders be sent to you, fax, email, phone? What information should be included in an order. What information should be included in a credit application. Do you have credit application forms or other forms the buyer needs? Where are they available online or will they need to be sent to the rep? Include any order forms in your orientation kit as printed forms too.

- Welcome your sales person as a representative, give him/her encouragement. Offer to be available if your rep has any questions. Let the rep know he is part of a team with your own sales people and yourself.

Be sure to include a letter with your CD or audio and a label with instructions on it. Reps do not want to receive an unlabeled CD in the mail with no information and no idea what it is for. Include a letter of explanation and stress why it is important, how easy it is to listen and why you provided an audio format so they can easily listen at their convenience. If the CD is an audio CD tell them to put it in a CD player. If it contains mp3 files, state clearly in the letter they can listen on a computer or in an MP3-CD player or copy to an MP3 player.

Provide information on your competition too. You do not want to bad-mouth your competition but reveal weaknesses in their product or marketing that your sales people can take advantage of. Stick to the facts and avoid hype or creative interpretation. Your rep will see through it and if he does not, the retail buyer will and he will lose interest in your products if he thinks you are trying to stretch the truth about your competition.

Your terms and conditions should also define the difference between a wholesaler, distributor, and representative so there is no confusion. Your rep may want to resell your product himself and he should understand your expectations and terms if he acts as a reseller. You also may want to explain in your audio the difference between a rep who talks a buyer into purchasing your product and a reseller or wholesaler who buys your product from you directly and sells it himself.

Your situation will depend on the product and your business so you may have other considerations or areas that must be defined. You would think reps would know the difference, but I have frequently been asked "how it works" with my company. Some reps are not the type of sales people who go to big chain retailers. Instead these reps meet school buyers and government agencies where they make a deal then buy from the vendor and deliver in person to the buyer, usually in small quantities. You must explain who is expected to provide support for such purchases. If you are selling for 50% off your retail price, then you may not want to provide customer support or installation assistance with your sales people for a sale the rep made. This must all be made clear to the rep before you find yourself in a sticky situation.

Territories

A rep usually sells within a territory. Some may sell even more locally, especially if the rep lives in a large city where he can find plenty of businesses.

Selling in a specific territory allows the rep to meet buyers personally, show product samples, and offer personal service when it is needed. There are formal sales territories which are actually left-overs from the old days of salesmen when they would drive to meet clients and all sales were face to face. It is very unusual for a rep to sell "everywhere" because he cannot reasonably travel from New York to California to demonstrate a few products. Reps also jealously guard their territories. If a rep can generate sales within a territory, then it is worthwhile to give that territory exclusively to that one rep as long as he is producing new sales. Sales territories are traditionally divided not by state but by region. These cross state boundaries.

The map on the following page shows roughly how territories are split up. For example, the Denver territory includes Wyoming, Utah, and Colorado. These boundaries are not absolute. If you give an exclusive territory to a rep, make sure you both understand what that territory covers.

Exclusive Territories

Exclusive territories are sales territories a rep sells to exclusively, meaning there are no other reps working that area.

You may give a rep the exclusive area of Southern California for example. Exclusivity is earned. If a rep shows he can do

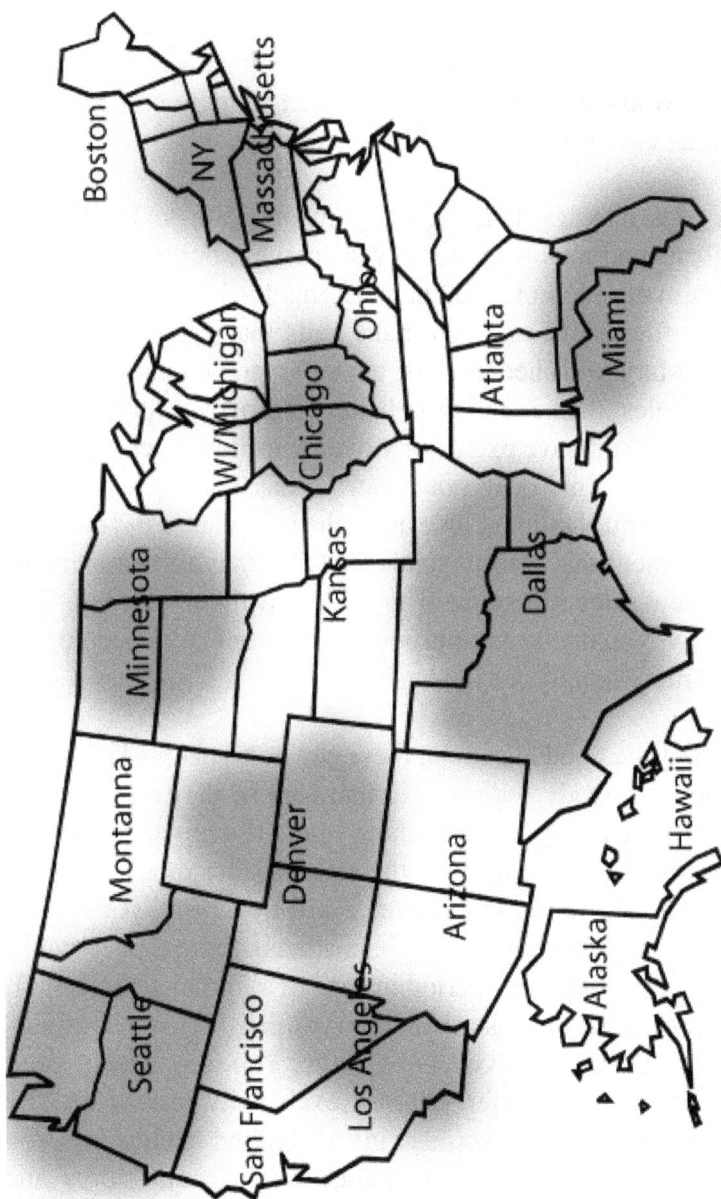

General Map Of Sales Territories

well in a territory and asks for exclusivity, then it is in your interest to give him exclusivity over that territory. It is not in your interest to give exclusivity to a rep just because he asks. If he is no good, you may be turning away other better reps who can represent your product to more companies or better companies.

A reps may work for a big firm or claim to have many clients and may even be very successful, but the only thing that matters is how well he performs for you. If John sits in his office alone and can make calls that get you business, but Mary with her team of ten salespeople cannot get you any sales, then John is the better salesperson for your line. John should have exclusivity over a territory because he has earned it. This does not mean he has lifelong exclusivity either. You should include an exclusivity clause in your sales agreement that clearly states exclusivity is earned and lack of new sales can cause it to be lost without warning. That allows you to give your product line to new sales people who are more hungry for the business.

It is also a good idea to let these new sales people know who you are already selling to in that area so they do not waste their time trying to sell to them again. If a rep does not have existing relationships with the major chain stores in his area, then he has no reason to even ask for exclusivity(assuming your product is targeted at chain stores). Start any rep with a trial or probationary period instead of a formal agreement. If he proves he can make sales, then you can discuss exclusivity. Remember, exclusivity is of value. You may change your percentages and offer 18% for exclusivity instead of 20% commissions. You can also award limited exclusivity. You may have one rep with exclusivity to chain stores and another with exclusivity to government agencies in the same area. Just make sure each knows he is limited in his range.

Remember, you are interviewing the rep for a job. He is working for you. You are not working for him. You do not have to give a bonus to your employee just because he asks for it. He has to earn it. Exclusivity is earned through making sales. If a rep cannot make sales, there is no reason to give him exclusivity.

Follow-Up

It is important to keep in contact with your sales people. You want them to keep your product line on top of their list of things to sell. Once a sale is made, it must be re-made over and over even to the same retail buyers. Anytime you receive a new order as the result of one of your reps, let him or her know immediately with a thank you note that also confirms you received the order. It is important to give positive feedback. You can achieve a great deal with just a little positive feedback. Let the rep know he is doing a good job and you are glad you two are working together. If you establish a pattern of thank you notes and miss one, your rep will feel slighted. On a subconscious level your rep is working hard to receive that positive reinforcement. Make sure you never fail to send an upbeat confirmation that thanks the rep for his hard work. Your reps may also use your commendations as proof to retail buyers that they are good at what they do and that the product is a hot seller.

If you have a number of top regional reps, you may consider publishing a newsletter. You can find newsletter templates on the web for your word processor. Simply update it with the latest "news" about your company and for each headline change it to be specific. "Fred the rep just closed a 1000 unit deal with XYZ Corp." or "XYZ Corp signs 1000 unit per month deal" and mention Fred in the first line of the article, then print and send this to Fred, and then change the headline and send another to Mary, etc. You may want to change the date for each person too. If Mary and Fred compare, then they have two different dates on their newsletters. Every rep gets a headline mention in your newsletter. You can print it on colored paper using your own desktop printer. When preparing this newsletter, remember that your rep may use it as a sales tool so limit all information in it to what you want a retail buyer to see. Keep it upbeat and make sure it shows how hot your product lines are and how they are growing. It does not have to be long, just one page front and back is enough.

Your newsletter can also be used to welcome new reps by writing up a short paragraph on their region and skills with a welcome-aboard story. You can also rate your reps by top sellers like a top 10 list(but don't give their names, you do not want any rep knowing who your other reps are by name). List new products, new shipping methods, changes that improve shipping times or ordering.

This newsletter is also a good place to include a box with one to three sales tips for all of your sales people. Pick tips that will help them sell your products. Think of it as a sales training refresher where you can repeat elements from your audio or give new ideas. Even if the information is in your audio or orientation packet, you need to keep reminding your sales reps about product benefits and other sales tips.

Trade Shows

Your rep will likely attend trade shows. You may also want to attend trade shows yourself. You can find a list of current trade shows listed by industry on our webpage in the appendix. You will need some professional graphics and signs to capture the attention of potential buyers at these shows too. Don't take the cheap route either. It only makes your product and company look cheap. See the appendix for a guide on how to obtain graphic design services at a good price. You can hire someone to design the graphics for you, then send the file to your local copy show which can print it out on foam core or another type of sign board. You can also send the digital files to any copy shop that is close to your rep so he can pick them up and avoid shipping anything.

What To Say To Reps

What is the etiquette for contacting a rep? Usually, you will find a rep on the Internet through a search service(see the link in the appendix which has these services listed). These give you a method to contact the rep, but that is only the first step.

Some reps may receive several contact requests each day and most of them are not suitable for their sales skills. They can be quickly overwhelmed so you must go beyond the default contact method. First, use the supplied contact method by the website. Usually that involves clicking a "contact the rep" button to send a message. Then immediately follow-up with an email that gives two paragraphs of information(no more) on you, your company, your product line. You can also give a link to a webpage where you have photos of your products and a summary along with more information. Whenever a rep asks a question, put the answer on this page. If one rep wants to know, the odds are good other reps will want to know too.

Allow the rep time to review your information. If you have

not received a response in 2-3 days, phone him. First, ask if it is a good time to talk about your product line or if you should call back. Then you can either talk or schedule a better time. Many reps do not even answer their own phones anymore. You are more likely to receive voicemail. You must be prepared for this and have a list of what you want to say in front of you. Address the rep by name, introduce yourself quickly and your company, state why you are calling and where you obtained the rep's information and mention if you already emailed and tell him what your product is. Tell the rep you would like to discuss his representing your products and want to schedule a call, give your phone number and name again and offer to be available any time. Also give your state. It may be difficult for a rep to call you back at a specific time and if you do not give your state, he may not know what time zone you are in so 5PM for him may be 8PM for you. If you do not hear back, it is acceptable to call again 5-7 days later. If you still do not receive a response and believe the rep is a good candidate for your products, send a letter in the mail and include your one-sheets.

How should you first contact a new rep? In the old days it was telephone only. Today, many reps let their voicemail pickup all calls so they do not answer the phone anyway. The best way is by both email and phone. The order depends on your product. If you have a product that you can quickly describe by phone which does not need a photo, then phone works. If your product is something complicated or that needs to be seen, then email is better as a first contact because you can include your one-sheet or a link to your website with photos.

You can email a rep, then in that email say you will call the next day when he has had a chance to look at the photo or one-sheet. If you call by phone first and leave a voicemail, then you should follow-up with an email letting the rep know you just left a voicemail message and give a link to your one-sheet or, if you spoke to the rep, thank the rep for talking to you and remind him how valuable his feedback was to you. Always end either an email or a phone message with some sort of call to action that encourages the rep to contact you to move forward or to "get this rolling".

How To Interview A Rep

Remember, a rep is applying for a job with you and you are trying to convince the rep your job is worth taking. You are evaluating each other. Neither is doing the other a favor. Not every rep will be right for your company. Some are inexperienced or even incompetent. Others are simply unfamiliar with your area of the market. You would not want a rep who usually sells clothing and jewelry to take on your industrial CNC modification board for manufacturing companies. That rep would have no idea who to talk to and could never speak the language of those companies. Such a rep would likely do more harm than good to your brand name.

You should ask questions, but you may not get a straight answer. If you ask a one person company how many reps they have, they can throw out any number. You have no way to verify if it is true or not. Most will be honest, but you must identify those who are not or who stretch the truth to gain your business.

- Look at the other product lines the rep's agency represents. Do they mesh with your products well? Some agencies have sections that specialize. One section may sell baby products and another home improvement products. Don't turn away a rep thinking he represents only baby products. If he has a multi-rep(more than one person working) agency then he may have someone who specializes in your market sector. Such splitting is a good indicator. It usually means the agency has plenty of business so they are good and they recognize the need to have dedicated sales people for different markets.

- How long has the rep been in sales? The answer is usually something like 10 or 20 years, but is it really true? Working in the sales department of XYZ company does not mean the rep worked in sales. He may have answered phones and taken orders. That is not sales. Sales means talking to customers face to face and walking away with a signed contract. It means contacting people who have not already expressed an interest in the product and stimulating their interest enough to purchase. It means studying sales books and attending sales seminars. Ask your sales rep what was the last book on sales he read. If he has no answer, that is a bad sign. If he says it was ten years ago, that is another bad sign. Good reps will always try to learn something new about sales as a business. So the real question is not how long have they been connected to sales, but how long have they been actively outside of an office doing face to face sales. There is also a difference between "been in the business" and "experience". The head sales person may have "been in the business" 20 years, but if 15 of those were answering order-line phones for a company, then that does not really count. Ask how long the agency has represented its top product lines. If they have been in business ten years but only represented the top lines two or three years, it can mean one of two things. Either they cannot keep accounts or they have not really been actively in this business for 20 years.

- Does the rep have contacts with the major chains likely to carry your product in the area? Find out what those chains are before calling the rep and ask specifically about the top chains or the businesses you want your product represented to.
- Is the management literate and intelligent? This seems obvious, but it is surprising how often the management fails to meet this simple test and even how frequently you find reps who could not graduate high school. Does the company have its own website? They should have a site even if it is not a sales site but a placeholder they use for email. These days, real companies have websites. Not having a website today is like a business not having a phone in the 1980's. Does the company use a free email account or worse an aol.com account for email? That is a sign of technical incompetence. If you are selling computer equipment or anything remotely technical, they may not be able to represent it effectively. Does the company have grammar or spelling errors on their website, correspondence or email to you? That's another bad sign. If their grammar is bad when talking with you, then it is bad with retail buyers. See the appendix to make sure your grammar is not driving away potential reps too.
- How committed to your product is the agency? Ask what will they do to promote it? Will they give your one-sheet to their sales people and have them leave it behind as an after-thought when their meeting with a retail buyer to discuss another product ends or will they actually talk to the retail buyer about your product and actively promote it? Will they setup meetings specifically to pitch your product, or will they throw your product in along with ten others

after pitching their leading lines?

- Does your rep send people to trade shows? What kind of displays do they have? Can they show your product by itself and demonstrate it or will it be on a table with 20 other products.

If during your discussion you find out the rep represents one of your competitors, ask if they are satisfied with the performance of that line. If not, maybe they will drop it in favor of yours. *If they are not selling it well, they also may not be doing an effective job representing it.* Many reps will not carry competing lines, but I see no problem with it. If a retail buyer is not interested in the competitor, maybe he will be interested in your line. The two lines may also be given to different sales people in the same agency.

When you are satisfied with a rep you should send him a rep kit(also called an orientation kit).

Your kit should contain:

- A product sample
- Your policy/terms sheet
- Your pricing sheet(the one for this rep's commission rate)
- Your one-sheet printed(enough copies to get your rep started, 15 is good)
- A CD-ROM with a pdf and jpg version of the one sheet so the rep can print it out or email it, and the MP3 audio of your sales guide. Don't depend on emailing it, but you can put it on a private webpage instead of sending a CD-ROM. Some reps may prefer to download everything.
- Any other marketing materials such as email formatted information, product specification sheets,

testimonial sheets, etc. If you have 100 testimonial letters from real customers, copy them and bind the copies in a book. That is a strong sales tool!

- Your audio orientation on CD-ROM (This can also be on your private webpage for reps.)
- A welcome letter thanking the rep for taking on your product line and explaining what is in the kit.

You can also send the welcome letter first and tell the rep to watch for your sample kit. This creates some anticipation so the rep will be more likely to go through the kit when it arrives and not stack it on a desk in the back of the office.

If your company has a catalog, include that too. It is a good idea to have a special private rep page on your website where all of this information is available. If a rep needs something and does not have it, he can open your webpage and see it on his laptop or print it out in his office.

In the past, some companies charged reps for samples. If you are confident in a rep selling your product, just send the samples and mark it off as a business expense. Serious reps dislike paying for a product sample. If you have a truly expensive product then they may have to make do with a photo or non functional demo model. If you are selling diamond rings, then you may want them to pay at least close to wholesale for the samples too. A reasonable rep will understand this for high value items that need to be seen when a photo is not enough.

If you have an inexpensive product, send several samples. The rep can give them away to potential buyers. If your company sells key-chain bottle-openers, for example, a sample taken home by a buyer can turn him from uninterested to interested when he uses it.

If you have a delicate or oddly shaped product, you need to provide an appropriate box. You never want your rep opening his car trunk to find your expensive item broken just before he walks into a meeting with a retail buyer. You also do not want your rep carrying an old beat up cardboard box to a meeting. It can be a sample case, an inexpensive foam lined case(you can pick up plastic pistol cases from Wal-Mart for $10) or a generic camera or equipment storage box or just a nice looking gift box(not brown cardboard). Check your local hobby store or gift shop for fancy boxes and paper. Put this in a larger box. The rep can transport using the larger box and take out the fancy box to show a buyer.

If your product does not show the product name, add a tag or other identifier to it with the name and product number.

Luggage tags, key tag labels, wire tie labels or other tags from an office supply store work well for this. You want a good quality plastic or leather tag that will not be easily pulled off of your product and will look nice. If you sell diamond rings and jewelry, your item may be shown to a buyer but the rep has no idea what item number it is which means he has trouble giving pricing or details. A tag will prevent this trouble and make it easy to identify the product name and item number. Keep a tag on all items that need them. If you are selling software or video's, then the information is already on the packaging. A good tag also makes it harder to lose small products. If you use a tag with a hook and loop fastener, your rep can remove it quickly during demonstrations.

Firing A Rep

What happens if a rep signs up two or three accounts, but

you have a falling out with the rep? You need to make some changes. You can contact the companies directly and let them know what is going on by simply telling them the rep no longer represents your company and you have a new rep. This proactive action will prevent you from losing an account and if the rep bad mouths you later, they will be more likely to believe you and see him as a bad apple. You should not give a lot of details. If you are asked, just say he was not working out for your company or not a personality match for your company so you are no longer using him. You never want to badmouth a rep because if the buyer has a good relationship with that rep, he may have second thoughts about you and your product line. Keep it business like and never make personal or inappropriate comments.

Starting Out

When you have a product the first thing you want to do is move it into big chain stores with big name reps. That is unrealistic because the first question any chain will ask is "who else is selling it" and when you are starting, the answer is no one. Start with smaller reps and let them get your product in a few small stores. Then move to bigger reps with bigger stores, then you will be ready for chains.

Smart reps will usually test your product on smaller stores. This gives them a feel for how well it will sell and they can also take this information to larger retail buyers as proof of the product's viability. If your product has been selling in other markets, let your rep know about it. He can use this information to gain those initial purchases. If your product has been selling at a store in your home city at a rate of 1000 units a month, that is something your rep needs to know even if that store is not in his area. It is much better for him to go to a retail buyer and give concrete numbers about a small store selling a lot of units than to admit no one has sold one of your products.

Online sales mean nothing to retail buyers. Having your product listed on Amazon.com also means nothing because anyone can have his product listed there. You need real sales numbers from retail stores to impress other retail stores or retail chains.

If you have one rep doing an amazing job, ask what he is doing. You may find a new approach to your product or a new method other reps can use.

Affiliate Programs

If you have a website, then you may have an affiliate program. This is a program where other websites can direct traffic to your website and if a sale results, they get paid a percentage. In some areas the percentage can be high like for downloadable products and software. Make sure the rep is not confused by this. You do not want your rep assuming he is making a 40% commission because your website lists that amount for affiliate sales. Some reps still do not understand the difference between a rep and an affiliate. A rep sells a product at a wholesale cost. An affiliate directs sales to you and you charge the customer full retail price. The higher commission amounts are only paid on the sale of full retail priced items through your website from referring websites. If your rep wants to be an affiliate, he can setup a special affiliate link on his website and visitors to his site can click it, if they purchase, the manufacturer's affiliate tracking software marks it as a sale in favor of the affiliate.

Problem Retailers

When you deal with a lot of people, eventually you will have a problem with someone. It may be a person who is not qualified to do the job and feels a lot of pressure or a person with a bad attitude. If you have had problems with a retail chain or a single store, whether it is non-payment or personal disagreements, make sure your rep for that area knows about it and knows to avoid that store or how to handle the situation.

It may be as simple as not talking to one employee and dealing with another instead. If you fail to do this, you are setting up your rep for a bad experience. You do not want your rep to be thrown out and blacklisted by the company and you do not want the retail store to talk badly about your product(false claims of poor sales or inferiority) to your rep.

If you change to a new rep or a rep with exclusivity over a territory, make sure he knows about any such bad apples and is clearly instructed to avoid them.

Tracking Results

Once you have a rep selling your product, your work is not over. You must track the sales and profits from each purchase. How much is a company ordering each month? How much per year? Are their orders staying the same, going up, or down? If this January's orders are up for most of your retailers and down for one, you must ask why. Your rep needs to contact this store. They may be hiding your product in the back, putting it on an aisle of dissimilar merchandise or simply not putting out more merchandise when it sells out.

You also want to track your costs and profits with the retailer including commissions to the rep. Just because you are selling a lot of product does not mean you are making money. Maybe you made a concession with a regional chain like offering free shipping. Is it worth selling to this retailer or are you wasting your time? How do these sales compare to others? If you are making $10 profit per sale from most of your sales and $3 profit from one retailer then is it really a good deal for you? Where is the money going? Does one retailer have expenses the other's do not like shipping or advertising costs not built into the price? Can you reduce those costs or raise your wholesale price? Can you change your packaging to include a coupon that draws customers directly to your website for additional sales? Can you stop selling some items to the store so consumers have to purchase replacement filters, refill kits, or other items directly from you and not from the store(so you can afford to sell at cost to the store).

You need to know the answers to these and other questions to keep a handle on your expenses and profits.

You need to know when a retailer is seeing less turnover. If you wait until the retailer stops ordering it will be much harder to make him place another order than it would have been to offer advice to improve sales of products he has in the warehouse or to provide new store displays that stimulate purchases.

When Talking To Reps

Call reps you want to carry your line in the mornings. This is an old sales trick. There are many logical reasons for making calls in the morning. Most sales people are in the office early in the morning when they can make calls and prepare for meetings or schedule meetings for the afternoon. Be aware of time differences. As I said before, your 8AM may be their 5AM. Some reps prefer to deal with voicemail only. If you call a couple of times and receive voicemail, leave a message.

Make your line sound hot. Sales reps receive many offers for products that are not suitable for their market and many useless product ideas from inventors and others who have no real product or a product that is unsellable. You need to make your product stand out and sound like an easy sell.

Tell the reps who else is buying your line. This shows them your product is in demand and buyers will be interested in it. If you have no buyers, then talk about your own store sales, your direct sales or your web sales. If your current year is better than last year, quote it. If your previous year was a bigger profit year, then quote those figures.

Use whatever makes your sales sound huge. If you can make a face to face deal with a local single owner store or two then go for it. Even if you have to give them some discounted merchandise at an introductory discount price, it gives you the chance to honestly say "Well, Bob's Superstore ordered 1000 units last week. I just wish I could reach all of the similar stores out there myself." Notice we said he ORDERED not that he bought. The manufacturer may have given Bob's Superstore 1000 free units to test sales. Make friends with local stores that have one owner. They can help you test point-of-sale displays, you can take photographs of your products in their stores, they may even give you advice on signage and packaging. It does not matter if you give them free product or discounted products. What matters is that you establish your product can sell in retail stores.

Make the potential of your product clear. If you are selling a new type of birthday candles, remind the rep how many party supply stores there are in the US or in his territory or how many birthday cakes are sold each year.

Show reps you have a good product or product line. Don't beg for a rep. You are offering reps an opportunity, they are not doing you a favor. Also remember, if they are not interested today, they may be interested in three or six months.

Ask a rep if he wants more information. You can then send an email with a link to your information page or mail copies of your one sheets. If you have a small and inexpensive product, you may go ahead and send samples. You can then follow-up in a few months.

Online Services

When you sign up for an online rep finder service, use a virtual credit card number. If you have ever had to file a fraudulent transaction report with your credit card company then you know what a headache it is to cancel your card and notify everyone using it for monthly charges. Some online services may not be legitimate or they may be reselling a database for another company you are already subscribed to, maybe without the first company knowing. The safest thing to do is to use a virtual credit card which is available from any reputable credit card company website for your sign-up payment.

This is a new card number generated just for you to use. If it is compromised, you can cancel this one number without affecting your main card. Set a limit on the amount and the expiration date. Some rep finder services charge high monthly fees. They may also ignore cancellation requests, or they try to stretch out response times to get an extra month out of you or charge unexpected cancellation fees. If you set a limit on the amount that can be charged to your virtual card number and set the expiration date of the card to one or two months ahead, you can prevent unauthorized charges and even disable the card anytime. This gives you control over your money and you never have to worry about a company charging your card for services after you canceled or them claiming they never received your cancellation notice. You can find a list of reputable and reviewed rep finder services using the link in the appendix.

Reps Charging Fees

Manufacturer's reps work for you, the vendor or importer. Never forget that. If someone claiming to be a rep contacts you and then "explains" that your product is new and they need a fee to "get started" or for marketing, then you know they are not a real rep but a consulting service pretending to be a rep. If you were interviewing a new office assistant and he said he was very interested in the job but would need a bonus up front so he could spend the extra time getting up to speed in your company would you hire him? No way! That is part of his job, just as it is part of the reps job to bring himself up to speed on your product and to do the footwork to sell it. If he expects you to pay him, then he does not expect to sell a single unit, so why would you pay him? If he were serious and good at selling, he would gladly take a sample of your product and one-sheet to some of his retailers, ones he thought of as test stores, and test out the product to see if it was worthwhile. When a "rep" tries to charge you, run away.

Calling Reps

When you start calling reps, start with the ones you feel are least likely to be matches. This will give you a chance to ask questions and to see what questions they ask. You can then prepare better answers for the reps you are more interested in.

When contacting reps, look at the lines they carry. A rep who sells to Target stores and deals with metal detectors, duffel bags, coolers, and sports products is unlikely to be interested in representing your lingerie line to the same stores. Reps have a certain area of interest. You would not go to your dentist for advice on a wart, would you? Retail buyers are the same way. They go to a camping rep for camping supplies and an underwear rep for underwear. When a store wants to buy lingerie, they do not ask the rep who sells them automotive parts either.

Look for a rep who sells your type of products, not just the rep who sells to a store you want to sell to.

Once you have a relationship with a major rep, you can ask him for advice. Ask what wholesaler represents your type of products or what wholesaler you could use that would make his job easier. Many companies prefer to buy from a wholesaler they already have a relationship with instead of adding a new vendor. Once you are available through that wholesaler, contact all of your reps and let them know your products are available through this wholesale company and remind them it may be easier to generate a sale if they mention this fact to a retail buyer.

Reps and Email

I am skeptical of anyone calling himself a rep if he does not have an email address that he checks at least daily. How good of a salesman can he be if he cannot use the tools of the trade. Not having an email address is like a salesman in the 1980's not having a telephone! I already said that didn't I? Well it is still true. When a buyer asks the rep to email sales numbers or a digital one-sheet, then what is the rep going to do? Reps who are still trying to live in the 70's or 80's cannot represent your company or your product effectively. Beware of reps who cannot use email.

Dead End Contacts

You will receive initial contacts through rep contact sites from reps who are interested in your product. They will respond to your posting or profile and say they are interested or need more information. You reply by email or even call and leave a voicemail message but never hear back. This is how it goes. Some reps are too busy, lose interest, or just enjoy playing the game and pretending to be interested when in truth they have no hope of representing your product because they are not good sales people.

Keep Your Own Records

You should always save your own notes in your own database with all contact information for every rep you use. Never depend on the website you used to find that person to provide his contact information when you need it. The site could have problems and lose the information, the rep may cancel his account, you may cancel your account or the information may be removed or changed by the rep later. When you contact a rep, copy and paste all of his or her information to a text file or your database tracking system so you will always have it available.

Sales Outside Retail

Not all reps sell to retail buyers. There are many reps who specialize in sales to schools, governments, and corporations.

If you have a high priced product that banks need, then there is a rep out there who sells to banks. If you have a product that is only of interest to machine tool makers, there is a rep who deals with industrial manufacturers. If you only use the rep to gain a lead and you do the final sale, it is well worth paying the rep a commission to keep him out there searching for more clients. You effectively have a team of salesmen working for free until they make a sale.

Suppose you worked for XYZ Corp for 10 years and in that time you learned that they used an Acme machine which needed a $5,000.00 add on board to manufacture widgets. The problem is the board has twenty features and your company only needed one so they were paying for a lot of features they never used. Now one day you realize you know enough about circuit design(or you hire someone who does) and you build your own board. You maybe even tested it on the Acme machine after hours didn't you...hmmmm? But, you now have a board that does the same job, which is a job many other companies need and you can have the boards manufactured, or even build them yourself, for $100 in parts. You find a rep who deals with companies *in your industry and related industries and he sells your board for $2000.00. You never have to do any marketing or calling. Let the reps do the work and you take the sales. It is a great system.*

Here is another idea. I worked at a company and they paid a machine shop to cut and build special cases for gauges. They purchased these gauge cases for $300 each. That was an outrageous amount, but they paid it and one of these gauges went on every machine that left the facility. Then, one of our engineers got smart. He used his home workshop to make these gauges himself. He quit the company and started selling the gauges back to the company full-time. He sold his units to the company for $200 and still made $150 profit on each one. The company used at least 20 each day.

Canada Sales

Many reps are in Canada. Canada is about 30% of the size of the US market but a great market nonetheless. One problem with Canadian sales is that it is a two language country, English and French. Packaging often needs to be in both languages. Your rep will tell you if this is needed. You can use the link in the appendix to find information on hiring translators to inexpensively translate your label into French if needed and even hire a French-Canadian to do it so the language is specific for Canadian-French.

Not all Canadian packaging must be in two languages. Some areas are predominantly English. If you sell to a chain store, it will need to have both languages. If you sell to regional or independents, it may not require both languages.

The bilingual requirement is a packaging and instruction booklet law in Canada. You can get around this by shipping to English speaking Canada only not the Province of Quebec. Most US consumer goods companies who ship to Canada from the US or other countries build the costs in therefore making the MSRP higher in Canada.

You will want to have one price sheet and terms list for Canada and another for the USA. Your Canada sheet will have higher MSRP prices and higher wholesale prices plus it may have them expressed in both US Dollars and Canadian Dollars. Make sure you consider the cost of shipping to Canada.

Shipping to Canada, or any foreign country, also involves customs duties. When you ship an item that is usually worth $20 or more, the customs department of the receiver country sends a bill to the receiver for customs taxes. Usually the receiver pays the duties but some retail buyers may ask you to pay these taxes. They can be expensive so you must understand how much they are before making any price agreements.

Foreign shipments also require additional shipping customs forms. These are an extra cost, but they take extra time to fill out.

Pricing Your Goods

You want one price for each product. You should not break prices down by quantity. You also want your wholesale price to be high so you do not end up taking a loss on any sale ever, even if you have to send a replacement shipment.

Some buyers, like Frys, charge a 7% backend(an extra discount the buyer takes off of your wholesaleprice) and Microcenter charges a 20% backend! By starting with a higher price, you take these extra charges into consideration. Your pricing should be based on a 50% mark up or close to it as the minimum. That means, the retailer can double the price paid to you for the retail price. So, if you have a product that sells for $20 at retail, your wholesale price would be $10 which is 50% of the retail price. This gives the buyer a 100% markup, or, in other words, his 50% margin. It also gives you room if the buyer wants to tack on a backend or advertising fee. You can offer specials like a holiday special, normal price $10 per unit, but if you order 1000 for the upcoming holiday, $7 per unit.

Correct:
>Widget Model #101 $10.00 Each Wholesale

Incorrect:
>Widget Model #101 $10.00 each for quantity 1-10, $9 each for quantity 11-50, $8 each for 51-100...

Some reps will tell you that you need a breakdown of price by quantity. If they need such a sheet then that is fine, give that rep quantity pricing but make sure you can make money at those prices. Your highest price will likely be higher than your single price too.

Your main sheet will have one price per product. The problem with multiple prices is: what happens when your rep is on the phone, with a buyer and he asks "how much?" The response is "*Well...there are different prices for different quantities and this and that and it's complicated...*". Never do that to your buyer. Set one price and when you are asked, you know what it is. No complicated tiers or deals. If the buyer is interested, he can then propose something complicated or ask how much of a price break he can get for ordering in quantity. Buyers also know the stated price is pretty much arbitrary. They know they can always ask for a lower price if they want and they negotiate.

There is another more important reason for setting one price. When you sell to a big chain or even an independent retailer, they buy to fill up their shelves in the first order then they buy weekly based on run rates. They do not buy based on quantity discounts. What they sell is what they will buy to keep up their inventory. They don't care about quantity discounts or buy two and get one free. That is a retail strategy, not a wholesale strategy.

You can throw your one big price in the buyer's lap, then when the buyer says, "Well, we need a 7% backend.", you smile and say, no problem, we will accept it gladly. You can do this because you started at a higher price than you might have otherwise. If the buyer received a complex price list and your lowest price was $5 for 10,000 units and your highest price was $18 each for 10 units, but your retail cost was $40, you would be in trouble if your buyer wanted to buy at $5 and then cut off 7% in backend fees for an initial order of 200 units. So never give out your *best* price. Give your one highest price and you can negotiate from there if needed.

Most of the time the buyer will take the stated price if he is interested, ask to negotiate or say no if he is not interested at any price. Below is an example of many major retail chain's terms. The company names have been changed, but these details are from real companies.

Example of some of the Major Chain Buying Information:

National Chain	Vendor Package (Backend)	Can Ship To Store	Warehouse Shipping Charge
BIG Drug Mart	14%	Yes	8% to 4 Locations
Rex Super Pharmacy	13%	Yes	12%
Big Office Supply	8%	Yes	N/A
BIG-Mart	14%	Yes	8%
Zul Chain	14%	No	Pack by Store by Location
Big Clothing Is Us	13%	Yes	N/A

In this chart, Vendor Package means the same as backend or the extra discount the retailer takes off of your wholesale price. It means they charge you for all their expenses like advertising. Warehouse costs means what they charge you for using THEIR warehouse if you do not ship directly to the stores. So to figure out what you make after all the expenses are tacked on to your wholesale price, you do this:

Your Wholesale Price - Commission Paid to Reps - Vendor Package - Warehouse Costs = Money You make Per Unit

If you have a $10 product with a MSRP of $20, and you pay a 20% commission to your rep, and the company you are selling to charges a 14% Vendor Package or backend with no warehouse fees it would look like this:

$10 - (20% commission) - (14% backend)
or
$10 - $2 - $1.40= $6.60 that you actually receive
You thought you were making $10, but when you sell to a big chain you are only making $6.60. This is why you should list your price at the maximum or closest to the 50% mark-up level. If you give a company a break, then you are not going to make a profit at the big chains when they take out a big chunk of your wholesale price to cover their expenses.

You also want to ship directly to stores to avoid the warehouse costs or raise your price enough to cover the expenses.

I usually choose odd value prices like $14.71 instead of $14.95. This is purely for psychological reasons. It looks like the number was calculated instead of being pulled out of the air.

The national chains look for the following:

- Margin: 50% off MSRP
- Displays: No Charge (Do you have store displays for your product?)
- Packaging: Bilingual (Eng./French) if selling in Canada
- Mark Down Money or Return Privileges for poor sellers
- Brand names
- Companies with proven retail sales

BIG COMPANY Inc. Pricing Sheet For Retail Outlets s in the USA ONLY   Revised 1/27/2010

- FOB origin(shipping point)(other methods may be acceptable on approval)

- Shipping costs paid by receiver

- Returns: Allowed minus restocking fee of 30% within 90 days of initial shipment(other arrangements by approval)

- Advertising Allowance: Not included (Chains that charge a Vendor Payment or Backend require approval)

- Delivery Times: Under 1000 units, 3-7 days. Over 1000 units, 1-2 weeks.

- All software is Windows/PC compatible(Not MacOSX).

- Orders do not have to be for even case amounts.

- Credit: Established businesses Net 30 on approval and with a securing credit card; Prepayment by credit card or check preferred.

- Questions?: Call JOHN SMITH, President BIG COMPANY Inc 000-000-0000

- Orders: Fax For Orders: 11-111-11111
    Email for emailed purchase orders: sales@bigcompany.website
    Address for Purchase Orders and Prepaid orders by postal mail:
        BIG COMPANY Inc
        123 Street
        Hollywood CA 00000

This is an example of what the first page of your printed price sheet might look like. Summarize your terms and give instructions on how to order.

Super Anti-Virus Software	
MSRP $29.95 Price Per Unit $14.56	Plus Shipping; Shipping FOB origin Package size 5 ¼ x 7 ½ x ½ ISBN: xxxxxxxxxxxxx Case Qty 100, Case Weight: 27 lbs Case Dimensions: 22" x 15" x 8"

Super Graphics Software	
MSRP $29.95 Price Per Unit $14.56	Plus Shipping; Shipping FOB origin Package size 5 ¼ x 7 ½ x ½ UPC: XXXXXXXXX Case Qty 100, Case Weight: 23 lbs Case Dimensions: 22" x 15" x 8"

Speak Spanish Now 2 disk set	
MSRP $29.95 Price Per Unit $14.71	Plus Shipping; Shipping FOB origin Package size 5 ¼ x 7 ½ x ½ ISBN: xxxxxxxxxxxxx Case Qty 100, Case Weight: 27 lbs Case Dimensions: 22" x 15" x 8"

Speak Canadian Now	
MSRP $19.95-34.95 (our web price $29.95) Price Per Unit $12.56	Plus Shipping; Shipping FOB origin Package size 5 ¼ x 7 ½ x ½ ISBN: xxxxxxxxxxxxx Case Qty 100, Case Weight: 23 lbs Case Dimensions: 22" x 15" x 8"

How To Water Plants DVD Video in envelope(also available in Amaray case)	
MSRP $12.95 to 24.95 Price Per Unit $8.95	Plus Shipping; Shipping FOB origin Package size 5 ¼ x 7 ½ x ½ ISBN: xxxxxxxxxx Case Qty 350, Case Weight: 21 lbs Case Dimensions: 21" x 6" x 11"

Contact your sales representative for terms, conditions, and any details.
Pricing is for the US only. Contact for Canada pricing. Pricing subject to change.

This is an example of what the second page of your printed price sheet might look like. Give product names, SKU or item number, one price, and shipping/package information.

Big Chains

Almost every manufacturer, inventor, or importer, wants his product in the big chain stores. Why shouldn't you? They have the money to buy your product, they have hundreds or thousands of stores which means if they only sell one unit a week at each store it can be thousands of sales for you.

If only it were that simple...........

A big chain retail store will want to know everything about your company. They will ask to see your financial information for recent years, they will ask about your market share, they will ask about your marketing efforts and much more. They want to know you are on the up-and-up, completely honest, and not someone who will tarnish their name. They want to make sure your product is safe and is not going to give them some recall headache because it has lead in it or it was poorly designed and they want to be confident they will not have lots of returns. They want to know what are you doing to market your product, what TV stations are you on, how much do you spend advertising, how many units are you selling? How much money does your company make? How big is your market?

If you have no market, they will not buy your product.

They have no interest in trying your product out and test marketing it for you. They want products that are sure winners from the start.

They want to know what name brands you can offer. As an example of how complex an agreement with any major chain can be, the Radio Shack contract is 58 pages long and it is one of the shorter ones.

The chains are more interested in how much money you will give them to get started than in making you money. You have to buy your way in and still make money.

Large retailers typically do not deal with small companies. You can sell your product through a wholesaler the big chains already work with if you can find out who those wholesalers are and if you can afford to deal with them. They are not much better than the chains and often have the same requirements. The big wholesalers also may require an up-front payment to be added to their system, then they charge you monthly fees for storing your product on their warehouse floor, then they do nothing to sell your product. It is your responsibility to convince retail chains to buy the product through the wholesaler.

If you have no market share or you are not spending six figures on advertising, they are unlikely to talk to you. The buyer at a big chain wants to know why someone would walk in the door of their store and ask for your product. If you are not spending a lot of money on national advertising, then no one is going to rush to XYZ Big Store to buy your product. That is not what the retail chains want to hear either.

You have surely seen TV commercials where a product is advertised and then at the end it says the product is available at Walgreens. Then ten minutes later you see the same commercial and now the product is available at Best Buy. Then, ten minutes later, it is available at Wal-Mart. This is a co-op advertising campaign. The details are beyond the scope of this book, however, the short version is this: you can advertise and the company will pick up part or all of the tab. Sometimes the advertising fee you pay a big chain can be recovered if you can meet the requirements of their co-op advertising program. They give you the money back, but you have to spend it all on advertising in advance.

You are better off targeting smaller independent stores and regional chains or chains of only two or three stores. Make this clear in your listing where you solicit reps. It will save both of you wasted time. Once you are established and making money, then you can decide if you want to go after big chains plus they will be more interested in your products when you have an established market share and you have proven your product can sell at the retail level.

Different Reps

What are the most common types of reps?

There are different types of reps. Some specialize, such as in computer hardware, or air conditioning, or automotive parts and accessories. Some are more general like convenience stores or gift shops. Usually the ones that are more general sell knickknack type products to gift shops, museum stores, and those odd little impulse items you see in drug stores and grocery stores. Next you have the bookstore sellers. No, they don't sell books. They sell other items to bookstores and frequently sell clothing that is branded with sports team logos(licensed of course) to these stores. Some sell health and food related items to drug stores and grocery stores. These can be an easier "in" than some of the bigger chains as long as you have some research or health label verifications to back up any claims.

Because this field is popular, you will see many reps with listings like this:

I supply bookstores, gift shops, toy stores,stationery, greeting card, pet stores, department stores, school supply, drug stores, convenience stores, schools, libraries.

Just because the rep lists a bookstore does not mean he can sell your book there. Look further into his profile. The above rep sells telephones and telecom items, tools, clothing and medical supplies. Just because a rep sells to pet store does not mean he sells pet products. The one above sells greeting cards and printed school supplies.

It is difficult to find a rep who represents books or authors. The problem is that if the rep convinces a bookstore or a bookstore chain(you can count those on one hand) to actually buy a certain book, there is no way to collect a commission unless the publisher is the only source. If the publisher is the only source then the major chains and small stores cannot order through regular wholesale outlets. If they cannot order through their normal channels, they will have no interest in buying the book. Even if the rep did make a sale, he is unlikely to try to make a second because he would not make enough money. You could never afford to publish in small quantities, give a 50% markup(doubling your wholesale price) to bookstores, and then give a 15% or 20% commission to the rep. You would make no money. Book sales are another animal altogether. You can find more information on book sales in the appendix link. Some exceptions are specialty books or collector books that are high value items and are treated like a product, not like a book.

Here are some other common categories. You can easily find reps who sell in these categories:

Books, educational toys, games, puzzles, software, gifts, stationery, school supplies, greeting cards, pet related lines, CDs, DVDs, home health care, impulse, cleaning products, hardware, housewares, electronics, paint sundries, electrical products, outdoor living, seasonal, hand tools, computer software, automotive, and business services.

If you have a product that is out of the ordinary or not commonly represented or something normally bought through wholesalers directly, then you may have a difficult item to sell. Software is a good example. If you go into any office supply store you see software. BUT, that software is by Microsoft, McAfee, and other big names. The cheaper stuff is nothing but rack filler bought from a wholesaler. You will notice that there are no independent company software titles, only brand names. This really cheats the customers because the customer cannot choose among some of the great software available, but the major chains simply do not sell software from independent companies.

You may want to take a close look at what these stores carry to make sure they would be interested in your product. Just because they carry software does not mean they will carry your software. Just because they carry kitchen pots and pans does not mean they will carry your pots and pans. If you look through their pots and pans and everything is a store brand or a major brand name, you really have no hope of breaking into that store. Try independent stores, catalogs, and other outlets. If you become big enough, then the chains may let you play ball with them.

Services

Some reps will represent services and others do not. If you want to sell a service then it needs to be something companies at least want to talk about. No one will hire you for accounting. They already have an accountant or an accounting department. See the link in the appendix for a recommended book that has more information on selling services to companies.

Selling Your Product Yourself

Don't be afraid to contact retail buyers yourself. You can purchase a list of contact names and numbers for retail stores and contact them yourself. You have nothing to lose. You can prepare a webpage with a summary and crafted sales pitch, email them and then call them after they have had a chance to look at your page. If they are interested you may get a sale. If not then you have lost nothing. You can find more information on this list of addresses in the appendix.

Don't leave it all up to your reps. You can call stores yourself, especially when you are starting out. If you can make the first two or three sales, then you can now use those when contacting other stores or reps by saying "Our products are sold at XYZ and ABC retailers in California."

Consultants

If a consultant contacts you and offers to act as a Manufacturer's Rep, but wants you to pay up front then you should ask what guarantees are included. This person is a consultant so he should be able to recognize a good product. If he can recognize a good product, he can sell it. If he knows a good product and can sell it then he can offer a guarantee of some sort.

He can offer to take you on for a discounted rate or for free until your first chain store sale is made. He can guarantee a chain store sale or if it does not happen he does not charge you anything. This is not outrageous either. It does not take that much to at least generate interest by a chain IF you have a product that will appeal to them. You only need a product and a one-sheet if you are in this boat.

Any rep who knows the business can tell immediately if your product will appeal to chains or not. If he is wishy-washy or says he can't guarantee anything or says "you never know" then he has no idea what he is doing. An experienced rep can look at a product and give you some idea whether or not retail chains will be interested.

You do not need fancy brochures printed on glossy paper with a pop-up fold out, expert "sales analysis"(whatever that is) or offers of nationwide distribution(an offer is not a guarantee!). Usually, any consultant promising nationwide distribution is really saying he will post your product on some seedy drop-ship company website so it is "available" to anyone who might order it. That does not mean anyone WILL order it, only that in theory it is available if a major buyer happens to drop by this nothing drop-shipper site and stumbles over your listing. Some of these consultants actually work for, or are affiliates for, the drop shipping company. They get a hefty commission for every manufacturer they sign up. In the end, you pay a drop-shipping site a lot of money for a listing no one sees and get no sales.

Any consultant who promotes these fancy trappings ahead of sales is trying to sell you a package-deal that makes him money and does nothing for you. If a consultant tries to sell you a big expensive package of services with no guarantees then run for the hills. He sees your product is a dud or he has no idea how to sell it but only wants to sell you a box full of fancy brochures, intangible consulting and "promotion" and advertising junk that will never help you sell your product.

If the consultant does not have enough confidence in your product to give a guarantee that he can make a sale of XX units in 30 days, then you should not have confidence in the consultant.

A consultant will tell you that you need a good label. It is true that a good label is critical. This is what the browsing consumer sees. If it is poorly designed, fails to say what the product does for the consumer, or is unappealing in any way, then you will never sell it anywhere. Some products may also have legal labeling requirements.

If you are a total newbie and you know your product label is bad and needs to be redesigned or your one-sheet is bad and you need a graphics expert to fix it, then by all means hire a consultant and pay for these services. But, don't get suckered into buying a lifelong "arrangement" with a consultant who promises big gains at some unspecified date in the future for your monthly payment or for a big retainer.

These firms have what is known as a "Customer Life Cycle" which means they know how much they can squeeze from a customer before he gives up and quits. It is frequently three to six months. They promise great gains, charge a high fee, pay a graphic designer a few dollars to make a brochure for you, then delay and delay with promises of, "We just talked to XYZ chain today and are waiting to hear back." for months until you realize nothing is happening. You feel like you have to keep paying them in case one of their contacted buyers comes through. The consultant does not tell you they did nothing more than mail a brochure to XYZ chain or leave a voicemail message and are "waiting" to hear back. Even worse, they may email copies of your brochure to their list of buyers. They can then claim they have contacted 120 buyers this week when in fact all of those messages were deleted as spam. They should never have to wait more than a week to hear back from a buyer either. The buyer is either interested or not interested.

Pay for specific products or services to be delivered at a specific time and always specify in writing specific results to be delivered by a specific date. Don't let a rep tell you "Oh, well we never know how long it will take to sell your product..." That is a lie. Any experienced rep can look at a product and generate a reasonable idea what the market for it is and how many sales calls it will take to sell it. Even if he is unsure, he can ask some of his buyers or other sales people in his organization to find out. If he asks buyers then he knows for sure what the interest level is in your new blue-widget-with-the-advanced-display-and-formable-legs.

If you pay a consultant/rep by credit card and agree to any ongoing payments(not a good idea), then use a virtual credit card number as I already described. With a virtual number you can cancel the card anytime to prevent new charges or you can limit the amount charged to it. If you have problems with the rep, cancel the virtual number through your credit card company's website. If you pay by check, your money is gone so never pay for everything up-front. Pay as you go for the services you receive even if it costs more in the long run.

Consignment Stores

One of the first question any retailer asks is "Who is selling your stuff now?" If the answer is no one, then that is the wrong answer. If you are a small manufacturer and need to be in a store before you can sell to your first big store, consider a consignment shop. Consignment shops sell items and pay you when they are sold.

You can find a list of shops in the US and Canada at
> http://consignmentshops.com/
> and
> http://consignmentstores.org/

Find a store that sells products in your category, contact them and send some products to that store. Now when you or your rep contacts a retail buyer, you can say your product is available through XYZ store in California and ABC store in Canada. It does not matter if the first unit has not yet sold, your products are on the shelves there. If your product is selling well, then use this in your marketing. For example, you might say: "Last week, we shipped 10 units to store X and two days later we had to ship another 20 units because the first batch sold out so fast." You don't have to mention that they were selling at cost or below MSRP if that is the case either.

Most of these shops deal with clothing and jewelry, some with furniture and other odd items. Any of them may take your product, especially if you provide a point of sale display or rack(assuming your product is small), or if you are willing to sell at your cost or outright give the product to the store for free to sell.

Getting in a chain store when you are new to retail is like

hitting a home run the first time you are ever up to bat. It is unlikely to happen. Bunt for smaller stores and when you have experience with those, then you have a history you can take to the bigger chains.

The Right Product

Is your product right for reps?

Not all retail products are good choices for a manufacturer's rep. Some are easy to sell and you will find many reps willing to take on your line. Some products are hard to sell and you may only find a few or none willing to represent your product. A good rule of thumb is to look for trade shows. If there is a trade show that would be a perfect place to display your product, then there are likely to be many reps who can represent your line. If you cannot find any trade shows where buyers and manufacturer's meet that would be appropriate for your product, then you are likely to have trouble finding any reps for your product and you may need to look at other promotion methods.

Research

I recommend researching your product by talking to reps before developing your product. Too many people develop a product, even begin manufacturing it, then hope to find a way to sell it. Find out what your reps can sell first, then develop a product that meets their needs.

If you already have a product, then you may be able to re-purpose your existing product or you may have to combine your existing product with another product.

Commission Sales Reps

You can also look at selling your product directly. Some products are better sold directly to the end user and may not be a good match for retail stores. You may do this through a website, through the use of affiliates, or by selling to walk-in traffic at your office.

Instead of selling at a wholesale rate to a retailer, you can sell at the wholesale rate to your sales rep who resells the product at full price directly to the end user. If you have a $30 product with a wholesale price of $15, you no longer have to pay a 20% commission. Instead, sell at $15 to your rep who sells your product directly and makes $15 profit per unit. This is a good option for products that may appeal to specific categories like libraries or dentist offices. A rep allows you to reach these diverse buyers who would never search for your product online and who you might have trouble reaching otherwise.

Conclusion

You now know much more than I did when I first started looking for a manufacturer's rep. You know how to deal with reps and what to expect. You know how to price your products, how to give support to reps, how to evaluate the suitability of your product for retail, the benefits and problems associated with retail chains and so much more.

The next step is to find your first rep. Go to the link in the appendix now to find your rep and start selling your product.

Good luck!

Appendix

In order to keep any references or links updated since the publication of this book, we have put all links and website recommendations on a private webpage.

Manufacturer's rep sources and recommendations, Background checks, hiring freelancers, and more -- Go to the below website now:

http://www.Manufacturing-Rep-Secrets.com/private.html

You can use this username and password if needed to access the above site:

Username: repbook

Password: repbook

GET YOUR FREE BONUS

Download your free audio bonus now at:

http://www.Manufacturing-Rep-Secrets.com/private.html

This audio program can help you in your marketing, your product label design, and all aspects of sales.

Sources For Manufacturer's Reps

How do you find a good manufacturer's rep? There are many websites offering search services, but some sites are better than others while all are expensive. We have prepared reviews of the top sites along with recommendations on our private webpage:

http://www.Manufacturing-Rep-Secrets.com/private.html

Grammar

It is important that you use proper grammar when creating your label, your sales materials, and when communicating with retail buyers and reps. Good reps will not work with you if you use bad grammar because they will assume you are ignorant and uneducated. They will not want to represent your product if you use bad grammar. You can find an excellent video based grammar course at

http:/www.SpeakEnglishLikeAGenius.com